Unintended Impacts of Redevelopment and Revitalization Efforts in Five Environmental Justice Communities

August 2006

Prepared by the

National Environmental Justice Advisory Council

a Federal Advisory Committee to the U.S. Environmental Protection Agency

Acknowledgments

The National Environmental Justice Advisory Council (NEJAC) acknowledges the efforts of the Unintended Impacts Work Group (UIWG) in preparing the initial draft of this report. The UIWG functioned as part of the former Waste and Facility Siting Subcommittee (WFSS) prior to its termination at the end of 2004. The NEJAC also acknowledges the communities and interviewees who participated in the UIWG's study. Environmental justice communities, regulatory organizations, environmental groups, and other interested parties worked long and hard on this study. The NEJAC thanks the people who reside in those five environmental justice communities for their continued engagement in the battle for equal justice. The staff of EPA's Office of Solid Waste and Emergency Response, especially Kent Benjamin, the UIWG's Designated Federal Officer, spent many hours meeting with the UIWG and prodding work products from them. Mr. Benjamin was ably assisted by EPA staff and EMS, Inc, which provided contractor support. Their efforts greatly assisted in the production of this report.

Disclaimer

This Report and recommendations have been written as part of the activities of the National Environmental Justice Advisory Council, a public advisory committee providing independent advice and recommendations on the issue of environmental justice to the Administrator and other officials of the United States Environmental Protection Agency (EPA).

This report has not been reviewed for approval by the EPA, and hence, its contents and recommendations do not necessarily represent the views and the policies of the Agency, nor of other agencies in the Executive Branch of the federal government.

National Environmental Justice Advisory Council Members

Richard Moore, Southwest Network for Environmental and Economic Justice (Chair)

Sue Briggum, Waste Management, Inc.

Charles "Chip" Collette, Florida Department of Environmental Protection

Stephen Etsitty, Navajo Nation Environmental Protection Agency

Tom Goldtooth, Indigenous Environmental Network

Eileen Guana, Southwestern Law School

Jodena Henneke, Texas Commission on Environmental Quality

Richard Lazarus, Georgetown University Law Center

Harold Mitchell, ReGenesis, Inc.

Juan Parras, De Madres a Madres, Inc.

Shankar Prasad, California Environmental Protection Agency

Andrew Sawyers, Maryland Department of the Environment

Wilma Subra, Southern Mutual Help Association

Connie Tucker, Southeast Community Research Center

Kenneth Warren, Wolf, Block, Schorr and Solis-Cohen

Benjamin Wilson, Beveridge & Diamond, P.C.

Charles Lee, Designated Federal Officer, U.S. EPA Office of Environmental Justice

Unintended Impacts Work Group Members

Michael J. Lythcott, President, The Lythcott Company

Robert "Bob" Collin, Associate Professor of Law, Senior Research Scholar, Center for Public Policy, Willamette University

Randy Gee, Environmental Specialist, Cherokee Nation Office of Environmental Services

Vincent "Butch" Wardlaw, Vice President for Communications Training Services, WPI

John Ridgway, Washington State Department of Ecology, Hazardous Waste & Toxics Reduction Program

Kent Benjamin, Designated Federal Officer, U.S. EPA Office of Solid Waste and Emergency Response

TABLE OF CONTENTS

National Environmental Justice Advisory Council Members..................................

Unintended Impacts Work Group Members...

Executive Summary i

Report Background... 1

**Reasons Why Gentrification and Displacement are
Environmental Justice Issues**.. 2

Role of the Waste Facility Siting Subcommittee (WFSS)................................. 4

Place Study Methodology.. 4
    Research Methods.. 6
    Challenges and Considerations.. 7

Findings and Recommendations... 9

Conclusion.. 18

APPENDIX

Place Study Summaries.. 21
    East Palo Alto, California 21
    Albina Community, Portland, Oregon 22
    Washington, D.C. Navy Yard 23
    Cherokee Nation in Oklahoma 23
    Pensacola, Florida 25

 **EPA**

**NATIONAL
ENVIRONMENTAL JUSTICE
ADVISORY COUNCIL**

August 10, 2006

The Honorable Stephen L. Johnson
Administrator
U.S. Environmental Protection Agency
1200 Pennsylvania Avenue, NW
Washington, DC 20460

Dear Administrator Johnson:

On behalf of the National Environmental Justice Advisory Council (NEJAC), I am pleased to submit the report, *Unintended Impacts of Redevelopment and Revitalization Efforts in Five Environmental Justice Communities* (August 2006), for the Agency's review. The report contains advice and recommendations on the unintended impacts of successful Brownfields cleanup, redevelopment and revitalization efforts.

EPA's Office of Solid Waste and Emergency Response (OSWER) requested that the NEJAC Waste and Facility Siting Subcommittee establish a work group to examine community concerns that unintended adverse impacts had resulted during the course of EPA's cleanup, redevelopment and revitalization efforts. The Unintended Impacts Work Group (UIWG) was also charged to draft advice and recommendations, regarding how EPA may address such concerns, for the NEJAC to consider.

To develop its draft advice and recommendations, the UIWG examined the following factors in five communities with environmental justice issues:

- Meaningful community involvement in the planning, cleanup, and revitalization process;
- Opportunities for current residents and businesses to maintain or increase a stake in the community;
- Equitable compensation for displaced property owners (if any displacement occurred);
- Sustained or improved property ownership stability and affordability; and
- Effects on health and the environment (noise, traffic, odors, and other cumulative impacts) from cleanup, redevelopment, and revitalization.

The NEJAC Executive Council conducted a Public Meeting on June 20-22, 2006 (Washington, DC) and deliberated upon the UIWG's draft report. Our deliberations resulted in the following major recommendations to EPA:

1. EPA should support the placement of EPA staff in local redevelopment and revitalization projects through the use of Intergovernmental Personnel Agreements.

2. All stakeholders should have the opportunity for *meaningful* involvement in redevelopment and revitalization projects.

3. During cleanup projects, EPA should make a concerted effort to implement a coordinated approach to public outreach for settings where redevelopment and revitalization issues are complex.

4. EPA should work aggressively to address the cumulative impacts of environmental problems present in environmental justice communities.

5. When appropriate, EPA should encourage an initial neighborhood demographic assessment and a projected impact assessment regarding displacement at the earliest possible time in a redevelopment or revitalization project. A similar assessment at the project's end should be carried out to measure changes and assess impacts. Such assessments may be facilitated as a requirement for EPA grant applications.

6. State, tribal, and federal environmental agencies should be encouraged to find creative ways to participate in local land use planning, process, and government. For example, where state and/or federal permits apply, conditional permit issuance may be encouraged.

This report represents an earnest effort to call EPA's attention to the challenging dynamics surrounding community revitalization efforts associated with brownfields redevelopment. The report cites efforts that have contributed to both positive and negative outcomes. As expected, the adverse impacts resulting from such efforts were unintended and, in most respects, beyond EPA's control. However, EPA may have the ability, through funding decisions, oversight, coordination, effective listening and communication, and other means, to constructively influence or mitigate these unintended adverse impacts. It is our hope that, through these recommendations, EPA can help foster redevelopment and revitalization practices that bestow the enormous promise of its Brownfields program to all people.

We truly appreciate the opportunity to provide advice and recommendations to you on this important issue. We want to acknowledge the efforts of the members of the Unintended Impacts Work Group. In addition, we want to thank OSWER for supporting the Unintended Impacts Work Group's work.

On behalf of the NEJAC, I look forward to your response to the report's advice and recommendations.

Sincerely,

Richard Moore /s/

Richard Moore
Chair

cc: Granta Nakayama, Assistant Administrator, OECA
Susan Bodine, Assistant Administrator, OSWER
Catherine McCabe, Deputy Assistant Administrator, OECA
Barry Hill, Director, OEJ
David Lloyd, Director, OBCR
Charles Lee, Associate Director, OEJ and NEJAC Designated Federal Officer
Kent Benjamin, EJ Coordinator, OSWER
Victoria Robinson, NEJAC Program Manager, EPA OEJ

Unintended Impacts of Redevelopment and Revitalization Efforts In Five Environmental Justice Communities

EXECUTIVE SUMMARY

The National Environmental Justice Advisory Council (NEJAC) is a formal federal advisory committee chartered pursuant to the Federal Advisory Committee Act (FACA) to provide advice and recommendations to the Administrator of the U.S. Environmental Protection Agency (EPA) on matters related to environmental justice. The report was initially prepared by the Unintended Impacts Work Group (UIWG) of the NEJAC's Waste Facility Siting Subcommittee (WFSS). The WFSS was sponsored by the EPA's Office of Solid Waste and Emergency Response (OSWER). Due to a change in the NEJAC's charter, the WFSS terminated its activities at the end of 2004. This report presents lessons learned regarding unintended impacts of successful brownfields cleanup, redevelopment and revitalization projects and makes recommendations to EPA, with particular emphasis on OSWER.

Unintended Impacts: Why Is This Important?

The nation is still in the early stages of urban environmentalism, a complex subject with intricate and important histories. The potential for unintended consequences for people, for place, and for policy is great. Solid wastes are accumulating everyday, combined with a century of relatively unchecked industrial waste that continue to pollute our land, air, and water on a bioregional basis. The wastes in our ecosystem respect no man-made boundary and the consequences of urban environmental intervention through policy or other actions, intended or not, affect us all.

For this reason, we must thoroughly and rigorously examine the unintended consequences of emerging urban cleanup policies. In essence, EPA may have unintentionally exacerbated historical gentrification and displacement. The UIWG heard from several community members that EPA funds have sometimes been used to support development at the expense of low-income residents. This is not the fault of any particular individual, program, or agency. It is not fair to suggest that federal redevelopment and revitalization programs are purposefully causing unintended impacts such as gentrification, displacement, and equity loss in environmental justice communities. However, the implementation of these well-intentioned and otherwise beneficial programs is having that net effect, underscoring the power of market dynamics. It also highlights an opportunity for EPA to exercise leadership to protect communities from unintended impacts.

Methodology

Members of the UIWG conducted research into issues of unintended impacts through a series of five "place studies." For the purposes of this report, the term "place study" describes the methodology used to assess the sites selected for research and analysis of unintended impacts. The UIWG used term "place study," instead of case study, to recognize the individual uniqueness of the ecology, culture, and history of the people in that place. Unlike case studies, these results may not be generalized from one place to another. They examined the dynamics of actual and/or perceived impacts of cleanup and revitalization projects on communities with environmental justice issues. For each location, the UIWG members:

- Reviewed available literature and Internet sites;
- Reviewed Census data from 1990 and 2000;
- Interviewed key stakeholders;
- Compiled and considered various forms of information provided by community stakeholders and NEJAC members with knowledge of the respective project sites;
- Analyzed and compared collected information with the intended outcomes of specified EPA programs;
- Determined formal findings by assessing impacts, focusing on trends, commonalities, and unique considerations; and
- Developed recommendations for EPA.

Additionally, the UIWG established a set of factors for determining how and to what extent cleanup-related activities and/or redevelopment activities impacted nearby environmental justice communities. The UIWG searched for both positive and negative impacts. The factors selected include:

- Meaningful community involvement;
- Opportunities for current residents and businesses;
- Equitable compensation for displaced property owners;
- Sustained or improved property ownership stability and affordability; and
- Effects on health and environment.

Limitations

There are significant limitations to the UIWG's review of unintended impacts. The study's scope was limited to successful brownfields, Superfund, and Base Realignment and Closure (BRAC) projects. These programs fall under the statutory authority and mandate of OSWER. Non-OSWER projects and sites were not considered. Therefore, the study assessed only a handful of sites. Due to the federal Paperwork Reduction Act, the UIWG surveyed only a limited number of stakeholders at each site. Additionally, the U.S. Census Bureau does not have data to assess displaced residents and locally-owned businesses. Neither does it have the data to adequately assess gentrification issues such as who has been displaced and why. For these reasons, the many dynamics that fuel displacement and gentrification were not within the scope of this study. Finally, funds and other resources available for the study were limited.

Recommendations

The dynamics of actual and/or perceived impacts of redevelopment and revitalization projects on environmental justice communities make up the heart of this report. Descriptions of five studies of environmental justice communities at the end of this report provide additional detail to support the report's findings and recommendations. These findings and recommendations were derived from observations common across various place studies or from particularly noteworthy observations from a single place study.

1. EPA should support the placement of EPA staff in local redevelopment and revitalization projects through the use of Intergovernmental Personnel Agreements.

2. All stakeholders should have the opportunity for *meaningful* involvement in redevelopment and revitalization projects.

3. During cleanup projects, EPA should make a concerted effort to implement a coordinated approach to public outreach for settings where redevelopment and revitalization issues are complex.

4. EPA should work aggressively to address the cumulative impacts of environmental problems present in environmental justice communities.

5. When appropriate, EPA should encourage an initial neighborhood demographic assessment and a projected impact assessment regarding displacement at the earliest possible time in a redevelopment or revitalization project. A similar assessment at the project's end should be carried out to measure changes and assess impacts. Such assessments may be facilitated as a requirement for EPA grant applications.

6. State, tribal, and federal environmental agencies should be encouraged to find creative ways to participate in local land use planning, process, and government. For example, where state and/or federal permits apply, conditional permit issuance may be encouraged.

Conclusion

The NEJAC recommends that EPA follow up on the issues identified by this study. Specifically, the NEJAC encourages EPA, through OSWER, to develop options to better address the issues and recommendations provided herein. Additional focus on many of the report's issues can be the subject of EPA's Brownfields Program forums and conferences. Likewise, affected community groups can help OSWER find practical solutions to the challenges cited within this report. Pilot projects to conduct community assessments regarding local demographics and displacement of residents and small, locally-owned businesses, both before and after redevelopment/revitalization efforts, can shed result in greater understanding of the issues raised by this report. Certainly, other ideas and resources are within the grasp of EPA to help minimize unintentional adverse impacts. As a result, greater support to the positive activities recognized by this report will result.

Unintended Impacts of Redevelopment and Revitalization Efforts In Five Environmental Justice Communities

BACKGROUND

For decades, environmentalists have been aware of the ecology of human habitation. For example, Aldo Leopold, noted environmentalist, scientist, and author, said, "everything is connected to everything else." Leopold's comments serve to underscore the findings of this report. Displacement, gentrification, public health, and land use concerns are all connected, directly or indirectly, to the EPA's mission of protecting public health and the environment. While each of the projects reviewed in this report included commendable efforts at community involvement, most fell short of achieving the type of meaningful community involvement that serves to help lift communities of color and/or low-income communities from the cycle of environmental injustice. When outcomes from cleanup and revitalization projects are assessed, EPA may have unintentionally exacerbated historical gentrification and displacement. EPA funds may have been used to continue private development at the expense of low-income residents. This is not the fault of any particular individual, program, or agency. It merely underscores the power of market dynamics and highlights an opportunity for EPA to exercise leadership in protecting communities from unintended impacts.

Environmental policy in urban areas across the United States is relatively new. Urban areas are complex. For at least a century, urban areas in the United States experienced unrestrained industrialization, with no environmental regulation and often no land use control. U.S. environmental movements have focused on unpopulated areas, not cities. In addition, U.S. environmental movements did not consider public health as a primary focus. Rather, they emphasized conservation, preservation of nature, and biodiversity. In addition to being the dynamic melting pot for new immigrants, cities became home to three waves of African Americans migrating north after the Civil War. These groups faced substantial discrimination in housing, employment, education, and municipal services. In addition, people of color and low-income people faced increased exposure to the pollution that accompanied industrialization.

Citizens living in urban, poor, and people-of-color communities are currently threatened by gentrification, displacement and equity loss on a scale unprecedented since the Urban Renewal movement of the 1960s. Community stakeholders have repeatedly voiced these concerns at National Environmental Justice Advisory Council (NEJAC) public comment periods and at the Environmental Justice Caucus meetings during EPA's annual National Brownfields Conferences.

Market forces appear to be the primary drivers of this phenomenon. Spurred by local government attempts to reclaim underutilized and derelict properties for productive uses, residents and businesses who once abandoned the urban core to the poor and underemployed now seek to return from the suburbs. By taking advantage of federal policies and programs, municipalities, urban planners and developers are accomplishing much of this largely beneficial "revitalization." However, from the perspective of gentrified and otherwise displaced residents and small businesses, it appears that the revitalization of their cities is being built on the back of the very citizens who suffered, in-place, through the times of abandonment and disinvestment. While these citizens are anxious to see their neighborhoods revitalized, they want to be able to continue living in their neighborhoods and participate in that revitalization.

In addition to facing tremendous displacement pressure, African Americans and other people of color also face difficult challenges in obtaining new housing within the same community (or elsewhere) after displacement. For example, when these populations are displaced they must often pay a disproportionately high percentage of income for housing. Moreover, they suffer the loss of important community culture.

While it is not fair to suggest that federal reuse, redevelopment and revitalization programs are the conscious or intentional cause of gentrification, displacement, and equity loss in environmental justice communities, it is apparent that the local implementation of these programs is having that net effect. These then become the *unintended impacts* of these well-intended and otherwise beneficial programs.

REASONS WHY GENTRIFICATION AND DISPLACEMENT ARE ENVIRONMENTAL JUSTICE ISSUES

Downtown renovation is now a matter of public policy in most U.S. cities. As the waves of new "gentry" move to large scale renovation projects in or near central business or warehouse districts, they come into direct contact with the current residents of these formerly forgotten places. Many of these older urban areas suffered from the industrialized waste practices of the past, and were not in high demand for residential development.[1] Low-income people, recent immigrants, and people of color who were unable to find or afford shelter elsewhere have established communities in these areas. The commodity of land being sold in the real estate market is more than a physical structure or piece of acreage. It is also a neighborhood, a political and cultural entity necessary for the sustainability of a community in that place. Gentrification has placed populations in urban areas in direct competition for inner city space with relatively powerful and privileged groups. Environmental cleanup of these formerly industrialized, now residential, communities can be a powerfully displacing force.

These issues have been a battleground for community preservation, racial equality, and housing affordability for decades. Some residents claimed that all major revenue corridors unabashedly redlined these neighborhoods. Redlining refers to the practice of drawing a red line around an area in which a financial institution will not make a loan. Redlining has a variety of forms, but the most common is the denial of loans. It can also take more subtle forms such as shorter repayment periods, higher interest rates, low loan-to-value ratios, and under-appraisal value of

---

[1] Yale Rabin, "Expulsive Zoning: The Inequitable Legacy of Euclid," in *Zoning and the American Dream: Promises Still to Keep*, eds. Charles M. Haar and Jerold S. Kayden, (American Planning Association, 1989).– discussing the intentional zoning practices of classifying land as industrial in African American urban areas. See also, pp. 27 -30 of ADDRESSING COMMUNITY CONCERNS; HOW ENVIRONMENTAL JUSTICE RELATES TO LAND USE PLANNING AND ZONING, National Academy of Public Administration, for the EPA (July 2003).

property. These activities have occurred in at least two of this report's place studies – Portland[2] and Pensacola.

Neighborhood vitality bears a direct relationship to the adequate supply of mortgage credit. Because of the high costs involved, very few people can afford to buy or repair a home with savings alone. In most instances, the neighborhoods denied credits are the same neighborhoods whose deposits were redlined by financial institutions. Therefore, the community residents cannot draw upon their own collective funds. In addition to economic effects, the decreased availability of institutional credit to a neighborhood has devastating psychological and sociological effects. Current homeowners, recognizing both the lower demand for housing in their neighborhood and a similar effect on property values realize that the sale of their homes will not yield a return equal to their investments. Owners of multi-family homes are no longer capable of refinancing their properties in order to secure revenue for further investment purposes. Therefore, homeowners and property managers keep maintenance and repair costs to a minimum, and the neighborhood deteriorates. Once speculators predominate as property owners, the levels of maintenance and rehabilitation plummet dramatically. More residents leave, and if unable to find a buyer, simply abandon the property. As abandonment rates increase, the neighborhood becomes less desirable, and a thriving neighborhood with sound housing stock becomes a collection of abandoned buildings and vacant lots.

EPA can use the Community Reinvestment Act (CRA), 12 U.S.C. 2901, to gauge the disinvestments of financial institutions in these neighborhoods. The CRA requires lending institutions to disclose their lending practices. Without knowledge of the past and present land use practices, neighborhood culture, and localized financial lending patterns, EPA may unintentionally exacerbate the displacement of low-income and people-of-color communities by its cleanup and redevelopment practices.

With the advent of successful environmental justice advocacy, EPA has broadened its urban focus beyond the issues of landfills, waste transfer stations, and air quality. The President's Council on Environmental Quality acknowledged that racial discrimination adversely affects urban poor and the quality of their environment in its annual report in 1971. The Sierra Club, the National Urban League, and other groups agreed, as stated during a 1979 conference in Detroit, Michigan:

> *People in cities bear the brunt of technological and urban sprawl – in pollution and resulting disease, auto–dominated transportation, inadequate housing, and dangerous, degraded neighborhoods. (CITY CARE: A National Conference on the Urban Environment)*

The dynamics of actual and/or perceived impacts of redevelopment and revitalization projects on environmental justice communities make up the heart of this report. It was alleged by some

---

[2] See video NORTHEAST PASSAGE: THE INNER CITY AND THE AMERICAN DREAM, feature length documentary film on gentrification in Portland, Oregon; www.northeastpassage.net/thefilm.html; Phil Busse, "Gimme Shelter: NAACP Forms Task Force to Stop Gentrification" the PORTLAND MERCURY vol. 1, No. 32, Jan.11 -17 2001.

interviewees that EPA did not vigorously engage urban areas until cleanup became mandated by law. Wastes had accumulated in urban areas to such an extent that they could no longer be ignored. The first Brownfields Programs were for adaptive reuse of urban spaces in order to preserve green spaces, primarily in white suburbs. In 1992, EPA published *Environmental Equity: Reducing Risk for All Communities.* Also in 1992, the Office of Environmental Justice (OEJ) was created at EPA. In 1994, President Clinton issued Executive Order 12898, making 11 federal agencies, including EPA, accountable for environmental justice.

The urban environmental problems identified by EPA, community groups, and environmental organizations in the 1970s never went away. Their impacts and risks began to noticeably accumulate, the accountability of state and federal agencies for environmental justice increased, but the programs for environmental protection remained as they were before urban interventions. The stage was set for unintended impacts.

ROLE OF THE WASTE FACILITY SITING SUBCOMMITTEE (WFSS)

The local impact of gentrification, displacement and equity loss is of critical concern to environmental justice communities and their advocates. NEJAC also is concerned about the implications of local decisions that have a predictable, negative effect on environmental justice communities nationwide. Based on citizen feedback to the NEJAC and EPA senior managers, OSWER requested that the WFSS conduct this research effort. The WFSS began discussing the issues of displacement and gentrification in the context of smart growth during the December 2000 NEJAC meeting in Arlington, Virginia. Between 2000 and 2002, the subcommittee refined the focus of this issue.

In the summer of 2002, the WFSS updated its strategic plan. A part of this plan called for the creation of an Unintended Impacts Work Group (UIWG) to examine and report findings for selected cleanup and revitalization projects around the country that are supported by federal, state, and local government funding and are considered "successful." The goal was to develop a report that includes recommendations designed to foster community-based planning approaches for the reuse of property that will promote sustainability, properly weigh impacts of cleanup, and foresee and forestall unintended consequences such as gentrification and displacement. Further, the UIWG critically analyzed how these projects affected environmental justice communities.

PLACE STUDY METHODOLOGY

The UIWG used the term "place study" to describe the methodology used to assess the sites selected for research and analysis of unintended impacts. The term "place study" was used instead of case study to recognize the individual uniqueness of the ecology, culture, and history of the people in that place. Unlike case studies, these results may not be generalized from one place to another. According to the UIWG members, the cutting-edge nature of their tasks and respect for the practice of communities speaking for themselves made "place study" a more accurate term.

A common reporting template and site-specific interview questionnaires were developed to assist with the examination of each place study. The combination of disciplined research methods and a common reporting framework resulted in a reasonable amount of rigor in the study process and greatly facilitated the analysis and comparison process once the place studies were complete. Lack of resources and time prevented a complete demographic analysis of other displacing, gentrifying forces (*e.g.*, redlining, U.S. Department of Housing and Urban Development's (HUD) Hope VI effort and cultural histories).

The diverse composition of UIWG members facilitated a fair-minded, evenhanded approach to selection, research, and analysis of unintended impacts resulting from federal cleanup projects. Directed by this plan, the UIWG established a set of factors to assist in determining how, and the extent to which, cleanup-related activities impacted nearby environmental justice communities. It is important to note that the UIWG searched for both positive and negative impacts. The factors selected included:

- Meaningful community involvement in the planning, cleanup, and revitalization process;
- Opportunities for current residents and businesses to maintain or increase a stake in the community;
- Equitable compensation for displaced property owners (if any displacement occurred);
- Sustained or improved property ownership stability and affordability; and
- Effects on health and the environment (noise, traffic, odors, and other cumulative impacts) from cleanup, redevelopment, and revitalization.

Future studies may develop their own factors as environmental research methods in urban areas

---

CLEANUP, REUSE, AND REDEVELOPMENT

Brownfields Site: With certain legal exclusions and additions, the term 'brownfields site' means real property, the expansion, redevelopment, or reuse of may be complicated by the presence or potential presence of a hazardous substance, pollutant, or contaminant.

Superfund Site: A Superfund site is any land in the United States that has been contaminated by hazardous waste and identified by EPA as a candidate for cleanup because it poses a risk to human health and/or the environment. There are tens of thousands of abandoned hazardous waste sites in our nation. At the core of the Superfund program is a system of identification and prioritization that allows the most dangerous sites and releases to be addressed within the confines of limited federal funding and human resources.

Base Realignment and Closure (BRAC) Site:
EPA: To sustain and streamline military readiness, the Department of Defense (DoD) recognized the need to close some installations and redefine the department's mission at others. DoD and Congress agreed on four rounds of BRAC actions in 1988, 1991, 1993 and 1995. A large portion of BRAC property was designated for transfer to other federal agencies or non-federal entities, such as states, tribes, local governments or private industries.

DoD: Base realignment and closure (BRAC) is the process DoD has previously used to reorganize its installation infrastructure to more efficiently and effectively support its forces, increase operational readiness and facilitate new ways of doing business. DoD anticipates that BRAC 2005 will build upon processes used in previous BRAC efforts.
funding and human resources.

continue to evolve. The underlying purpose of this study was to identify the lessons learned from successful programs and, based upon them, make recommendations to EPA.

Members deliberated for a considerable period before selecting the final place study locations included in this report. A variety of selection factors were considered including quality of available information, existence of an environmental justice community in the study area, personal knowledge of the place study location, and the type of EPA-sponsored program involved in the cleanup location, *i.e.*, Brownfields Program, Superfund, Brownfields Showcase, or other grant programs. The UIWG reviewed a list of 125 projects before narrowing the field down to five place studies. The following text box provides descriptions of key terms associated with the above programs.

The five sites selected for this study offer demographic and geographic diversity in the following ways:

- Five different EPA Regions;
- Urban and rural settings;
- Multiple grant programs;
- Economically diverse stakeholder groups; and
- Racially and ethnically diverse community residents including African-Americans, Latinos, and Native Americans.

Research Methods: To achieve the assigned goal, the UIWG carefully deliberated on the methodology used throughout this report. Members of the Work Group considered the methodology extremely important because it established the underpinnings for how the research would be conducted as well as the final basis for the findings and recommendations to EPA. UIWG's methodology included:

- Selecting, researching, and analyzing five place study locations around the United States;
- Reviewing available literature and Internet sites;
- Reviewing Census data from 1990 and 2000;
- Conducting interviews with key stakeholders;
- Compiling and considering various forms of oral and written information provided by community stakeholders and NEJAC members with knowledge of the respective project sites;
- Analyzing and comparing information collected against intended outcomes of grant programs;
- Determining formal findings by assessing quantitative and qualitative impacts, focusing on trends, commonalities, and unique considerations; and
- Based on these findings, developing specific, defensible, and achievable recommendations for EPA.

Figure 1, below, provides a comparative description of the diverse nature of selected projects.

Challenges and Considerations: The study faced considerable challenges in establishing defensible methodology. These challenges included selection from a vast number of relevant projects, limited information on certain sites of high interest, resource challenges, and identifying commonalities across a broad range of unique study locations.

The use of Census data was a particular challenge. The Census is constitutionally mandated to be conducted every 10 years, so its results are often out-of-date and do not fit into project timeframes. In addition, Census data is not collected in a way that is designed to confirm or disprove gentrification. For example, the 2000 Census has much greater detail about the broad variety of races and local multiethnic populations than prior Census data. These variations challenge comparisons regarding place study sites that were receiving brownfields redevelopment and revitalization attention before 2000. Because of categorical and methodological changes with respect to race between 1990 and 2000, the Census data is not completely comparable between these two decades. The Census is known to have undercounts of vulnerable populations of interest to this project such as homeless people, non-whites, and undocumented persons.

Figure 1 – Place Study Matrix

Location Selected	Description	EPA or Federally Sponsored Program	Demographics
East Palo Alto, California	City-wide, multi-funded cleanup and revitalization projects for community, business, and residential uses. Urban setting.	Brownfields Pilot Brownfields Showcase Brownfields Development HUD Brownfields Economic Development (BEDI)	2000: 77.6% minority 1990: 73.7% minority
Albina Community, Portland, Oregon	Cleanup and mixed use development project to improve water quality, preserve open spaces, and create new jobs and housing. Urban setting.	Brownfields Development Brownfields Showcase	2000: 45.5% minority 1990: 56.0% minority
Washington Navy Yard, Washington, D.C.	Multi-funded cleanup and revitalization project. Urban setting.	Base Realignment and Closure (BRAC) Superfund	2000: 96.7% minority 1990: 82.4% minority
Cherokee Nation in Oklahoma	Pilot assessment project conducted in tribal lands. Rural, tribal setting.	Brownfields Pilot	2000: 35.6% minority 1990: 27.9%
Pensacola, Florida	Large-scale relocation project.	Superfund/Superfund Redevelopment Pilot	2000: 95.7% minority 1990: Block Data Not Available

Further, many of the studied dynamics such as gentrification and displacement are very hard to measure because the Census may show some amount of evidence of these inner-city problems, but the data does not reflect exactly why population shifts occur. The Census data does not count people in ways to accurately gauge why people live where they do, why they move relative to environmental contamination or projects, or where they move. Without up-to-date, accurate, population information, it was difficult to validate cause and effect from any one federal, state or local program, policy, or project. Any agency or community will face these same challenges of data limitations. In the event of relocation, an accurate assessment of local demographic information, before and after such efforts are implemented, is necessary. This can help gauge and control unintended impacts.

While Census data is inexpensive and somewhat accessible, it is complicated and often intimidating to the layperson to use. For that matter, government officials at all levels typically lack experience in understanding and using Census data. Census data also does not measure issues of vulnerability and housing discrimination. Further, communities often lack access to, and awareness of, local zoning decisions.

The problems with Census data are serious when trying to examine unintended consequences such as gentrification/displacement in communities with vulnerable populations. Urban areas with denser populations may be affected even more from redevelopment and revitalization cleanup policies, especially if they become of part of already existing trends of gentrification and displacement. If policy makers are unaware of consequences, whether by population undercounting, dilution of salient race demographics, or disappearance (due to undercounting) of people from public housing, then it is easy to claim that consequences to these populations were not intended. Many cities have contested the Census for the undercounting of minority populations.

Another challenge in the use of Census data regarding these place studies and disenfranchised populations is dilution. Dilution occurs when a particular sub-population (*e.g.*, a 'community' within a relatively small geographic area such as a few blocks or of a particular economic class or race/ethnicity) is compared to a much larger area or demographic population. When dilution happens, the small area or group of interest looks to be comparatively insignificant, and thus it receives little or no attention. Yet, this is where some of the most notable and troubling problems of inequity, dislocation and gentrification often exist in the most extreme form. The information derived from larger census tracts and block groups may dilute the actual presence or absence of racial groups, low-income groups and others. Undercounting within these areas makes the dilution impact even worse.

FINDINGS AND RECOMMENDATIONS

This section presents the report's findings and recommendations. The report's findings are based on the UIWG's place studies. They present observations common to several place studies, as well as important observations that may be unique to a single study. Based upon these findings, the NEJAC makes the following recommendations:

1. EPA should support the placement of EPA staff in local redevelopment and revitalization projects through the use of Intergovernmental Personnel Agreements.

2. All stakeholders should have the opportunity for *meaningful* involvement in redevelopment and revitalization projects.

3. During cleanup projects, EPA should make a concerted effort to implement a coordinated approach to public outreach for settings where redevelopment and revitalization issues are complex.

4. EPA should work aggressively to address the cumulative impacts of environmental problems present in environmental justice communities.

5. When appropriate, EPA should encourage an initial neighborhood demographic assessment and a projected impact assessment regarding displacement at the earliest possible time in a redevelopment or revitalization project. A similar assessment at the project's end should be carried out to measure changes and assess impacts. Such assessments may be facilitated as a requirement for EPA grant applications.

6. State, tribal, and federal environmental agencies should be encouraged to find creative ways to participate in local land use planning, process, and government. For example, where state and/or federal permits apply, conditional permit issuance may be encouraged.

FINDING #1: **Community involvement and progress at cleanup and revitalization sites are significantly enhanced when dedicated, full-time cleanup and public involvement experts work for the local jurisdiction on a long-term basis.**

In East Palo Alto, California and at the Navy Yard in Washington, D.C., EPA's regional offices provided federal staffs. In Pensacola, a different model was applied where a private-sector consultant was available directly to the community through the Technical Assistance Grant (TAG) program. These experts have a solid understanding of relevant environmental laws, cleanup logistics and the inter-relationships between multiple agencies that are involved with cleanups. They also facilitated public education and involvement efforts regarding site redevelopment and revitalization. They worked directly for city managers and staff, not EPA. These workers developed relationships with counterparts in other agencies and they understood their respective roles, resources, jurisdictions and political dynamics. It also was clear that dedicated expertise applied not only to full-time status and multi-year commitments from EPA, but it equally applied to the expert's positive and conscientious attitude toward the diverse stakeholders involved. This kind of resource is invaluable for providing stronger links between

EPA, local governments, and local residents and businesses. This is a successful element and effort by all accounts.

The duties of such an advisor should include educating the community about the redevelopment and revitalization process, including short- and long-term implications for the nearby neighbors. Meaningful community involvement should start well before decisions are made during the planning and implementation phases of the redevelopment and revitalization effort. Experience from Pensacola, Florida suggests that an expanded TAG program could help communities secure the services of such an advisor. In low-trust environments, an advisor that is hired directly by, and is responsible to, the community may more easily enable the community to "ramp up" their learning curve and participate more meaningfully in the process.

RECOMMENDATION #1: EPA should encourage the placement of EPA staff in local redevelopment and revitalization projects through, for example, the use of Intergovernmental Personnel Agreements (IPA).

Through the Brownfields Showcase Communities Project, federal government staff have been placed in various state and local agencies for extended periods of time. In these roles, the staff serve as a liaison among various federal agencies and programs to enhance the efficient access to federal resources. Often, these placements help to give voice to community concerns about adverse environmental impacts by providing technical expertise and a dedicated resource. This practice has yielded great benefits to communities, such as East Palo Alto, California. This practice should be expanded to service more communities nationwide.

However, certain considerations should be taken into account before this program is expanded. First of all, these individuals should want to be in such a position; it is not a job to simply be assigned. These individuals need to possess outstanding interests and skills with public relations, cultural awareness, understanding federal grant processes, environmental assessment, and cleanup requirements and processes. They also need to have a true interest and skill for working with relatively diverse stakeholders. Such experts must be willing to act in the position for an extended period of time (possibly years) if it is to be successful.

Specific to this recommendation, EPA should plan early to ensure that funding for this resource is available and utilized throughout a brownfields redevelopment and revitalization effort. Early budget requests and allocation is paramount to implement this recommendation. Placement of such staff should happen as soon as a brownfields site has been selected. Likewise, community stakeholders should be looking for this resource early and remind EPA of the need and value that comes from such individuals. Additionally, EPA should hire or support the hiring of local expertise to be available directly to community groups (as opposed to local government entities). Such expertise may include toxicologists, environmental consultants, community outreach/facilitation firms, and environmental scientists who can be technical advocates for the residents and local businesses in the area. Early and on-going funding for these local government/community tools is critical for long-term success and more equitable community involvement.

EPA's use of IPAs has been very successful. The continuation of this practice will increase the likelihood of achieving environmental justice solutions which are sustainable over the long-term, especially in financially distressed communities. The NEJAC commends EPA's use of IPAs in brownfields redevelopment and revitalization projects and strongly encourages the Agency to enhance this practice.

FINDING #2: **Redevelopment and revitalization are significant issues for environmental justice communities and all stakeholders, and warrant *meaningful* community involvement throughout the life of a project.**

In some place study communities, such as Pensacola, Florida and the Albina section of Portland, Oregon, community members' expectations to participate in the cleanup and redevelopment process were unfulfilled. For example, the Albina community expected to be meaningfully involved after the City of Portland was awarded a brownfields assessment grant. They expected that their participation would influence and potentially alter the outcome of the project. In the Washington Navy Yard, meaningful community involvement was less effective because the community had a limited capacity to review and comprehend technical data. Other communities were more meaningfully involved as a result of the brownfields projects. For example, communities in East Palo Alto, California were provided multiple opportunities for public involvement through advisory committees and public meetings.

Environmental justice communities can be involved in redevelopment and revitalization in many ways. Their involvement can be empowering, but it also can be displacing. EPA and other stakeholders may have overlooked some source of emissions, or other issues, requiring the reassessment of a brownfields site. Treatment of communities in the waste removal process is an issue of fundamental fairness and human dignity. While many cities embrace brownfields redevelopment, their commitment to meaningfully involving affected communities has varied. Ensuring meaningful community involvement has often been a struggle for communities and grassroots environmental justice groups. One example is the Environmental Justice Action Group (EJAG). In Portland, EJAG worked with communities to achieve meaningful involvement as well as to address other environmental justice issues at the local, state, and national level. From the community perspective, one frustrating aspect of the brownfields process was, and continues to be, the fact that some brownfields properties were assessed but no actual, physical improvement occurred (see Albina place study). Another general concern was that clean up standards were set to industrial levels, rather than residential ones. Without the meaningful participation of the residents of a given community, these types of concerns would not be identified and addressed.

Stakeholders have common and important questions about cleanup standards, liability issues and cumulative impacts that need to be considered early and addressed throughout the cleanup effort. The potential negative consequences of a redevelopment and revitalization effort can be serious, particularly when there are other sources of pollution close by and relocation and/or displacement factors are already at play in the area.

In some communities where gentrification and displacement of environmental justice communities have occurred, the environmental problems of cumulative risks, poorly regulated industrial neighbors, and decaying infrastructure continue to affect new residents. In a recent environmental justice training in Portland, Oregon conducted by the Multnomah County Health Department, environmental justice organizers commented on these issues. Such urban areas will continue to pose environmental problems for EPA and state environmental agencies.

The value of meaningful community involvement has been recognized in tribal settings as well. With meaningful community involvement, tribes can respect the overall interests of the community, and promote and protect tribal sovereignty. As tribes continue to participate in redevelopment and revitalization grant programs, full public involvement (both tribal and non-tribal) should be a goal of the program.

RECOMMENDATION #2: **All stakeholders should have the opportunity for *meaningful* involvement in redevelopment and revitalization projects.**

All stakeholders to the redevelopment and revitalization process benefit from full public involvement. Accomplishing this goal requires aggressive outreach by federal, state, and local sponsors to overcome barriers to public involvement found in communities of color. A targeted education process or the assignment of community-controlled development experts must accompany the promise of meaningful community involvement.

Community activists must have an educated perspective to decide if brownfields programs will provide hope and opportunity to their distressed neighborhoods, or whether they will exacerbate environmental contamination and/or provide little or no opportunity for their own families to benefit proportionately. Brownfields redevelopment is a big business. Profits are generally more important to brownfields entrepreneurs than community concerns about displacement or reduced cleanup standards. In fact, at EPA's 2004 National Brownfields Conference, developers reinforced this notion by highlighting their perspective that in order for communities to be "players" in the redevelopment and revitalization process, they need to be financially vested in the process. This view clearly speaks to the need for EPA intervention to ensure meaningful community involvement irrespective of financial status.

Our place studies underscored the need to redouble efforts at meaningful community involvement. Keys to meaningful involvement include (1) making multi-agency public outreach programs seamless and comprehensive such that communities are not forced to wade through bureaucracy after bureaucracy, (2) full funding of outreach staff in community locations, (3) educating community leaders on the redevelopment and revitalization process and its impacts, (4) addressing community barriers to leveraging outreach opportunities, and (5) providing adequate funds that will enable the community to hire their own technical experts, perhaps using the TAG model.

In the tribal context, NEJAC has already begun to address this notion through the report, *Meaningful Involvement and Fair Treatment by Tribal Environmental Regulatory Programs,* developed by the NEJAC Indigenous Peoples Subcommittee. Boards and commissions to address environmental concerns and development of environmental statutes, such as the Cherokee Nation Environmental Protection Commission, can assist in increasing public participation among tribal and non-tribal entities.

FINDING #3: **Cleanup projects benefit from a coordinated approach to public outreach.**

Federal, state, and local government-sponsored projects tend to view their work on a project-by-project basis. These projects are separated by specific lines of authority, responsibility, and funding that are generally clear to government agencies and some individuals. However, communities tend to view these projects as a seamless series of government-sponsored projects with unclear lines of authority, responsibility, and/or funding. These divergent vantage points lead to frustration on the part of environmental justice communities because they are often unable to obtain clear, timely, reliable, or consolidated information about all the cleanup/revitalization projects impacting their communities.

RECOMMENDATION #3: **During cleanup projects, EPA should make a concerted effort to implement a coordinated approach to public outreach for settings where redevelopment and revitalization issues are complex.**

Federal, state, and local sponsors of cleanup and revitalization projects must work closely to provide seamless community outreach by seeking to break down a community's understanding of the cumulative effects of cleanup projects. A "clearinghouse" approach to public outreach will provide significant support to communities by consolidating all relevant information. Further, a public outreach clearinghouse will shift the responsibility to provide information to the government. An effort of this nature could expand beyond federal government involvement at cleanup sites by providing information regarding local zoning decisions, a coherent overview of all related cleanup activities, and other relevant background. The net effect will be increased transparency, reduced bureaucracy, and more empowered citizens.

FINDING #4: **There is continuing concern among environmental justice communities regarding cumulative impacts of environmental problems.**

Current and past potential risks associated with redeveloped sites are often not fully considered as the redevelopment and revitalization process proceeds. Full engagement of the community is essential to generating a more comprehensive understanding of actual and potential risks that could occur as a result of the redevelopment and revitalization process. For example, in the Washington Navy Yard place study, several ongoing projects hold the potential for cumulative environmental impacts to nearby communities. These impacts include the cleanup of the Navy Yard, considerable construction activities for a nearby Hope VI housing project, and the Anacostia Waterfront development project. In East Palo Alto, the community and stakeholders considered multiple nearby-contaminated sites, geographically and historically, before the redevelopment and revitalization decisions were made and implemented. In Portland, the Multnomah County Health Department has focused considerable attention to the issue of cumulative risks and impacts. Although methods to assess and address cumulative risks and impacts may be beyond the current ability or authority of federal and state environmental agencies, they have been discussed recently in the NEJAC report, *Ensuring Risk Reduction in Communities with Multiple Stressors: Environmental Justice and Cumulative Risks/Impacts* (December 2004).

This finding is important in the redevelopment and revitalization context because it underscores the need to clean up a site as thoroughly as possible to decrease the accumulation of environmental impacts in a local area. Sites that are cleaned up to industrial standards or not cleaned up at all contribute to the sum of accumulated environmental impacts. If a group of contaminated sites are located near a proposed redevelopment and revitalization effort, the cumulative impacts of those sites on the residents and local workforce may not receive adequate consideration. A site-by-site assessment often ignores the potential synergistic and cumulative effect of multiple sources of contamination in proximity to each other.

RECOMMENDATION #4: EPA should work aggressively to address the cumulative impacts of environmental problems present in environmental justice communities.

This report builds on two other NEJAC reports – *Advancing Environmental Justice through Pollution Prevention* (June 2003) and *Ensuring Risk Reduction in Communities with Multiple Stressors: Environmental Justice and Cumulative Risks/Impacts* (December 2004).

Cumulative impacts concern EPA because they erode environmental protection and threaten public health, safety, and welfare. They cross all media – land, air, and water. Independently, media-specific impacts have been the focus of EPA's work for years. However, if the combined, accumulating impacts of industrial, commercial, and municipal development continue to be ignored, the synergistic problems will only get worse. The cleanup of past industrial practices must be thorough and safe for all vulnerable populations.

By far, the populations most impacted by brownfields decisions are those who live, work, play, or worship near a contaminated site. These people are already in areas of high pollutant loading, with generally higher rates of asthma (*e.g.* Albina). Vulnerable populations like pregnant women, the elderly, children, and those individuals with preexisting health problems are at increased risk. In many environmental justice communities, a brownfield site may be the only park-like setting available, so it can attract some of the most vulnerable populations.

To the extent members of the community are forced to leave because of increased housing costs, the community loses a piece of its fabric, and sometimes knowledge of history and culture. This adverse impact needs to be addressed as part of a cumulative assessment. The sense of identity common to many environmental justice communities is threatened when communities are displaced.

The National Environmental Policy Act (NEPA), through its environmental impact statement (EIS), is the primary and current federal statutory authority/process for considering cumulative effects. However, EISs are often inadequate to address environmental justice, gentrification and dislocation issues. In the main, EISs have not considered the more social or selective impacts associated with these issues. When determining the scope of issues to be addressed during the preparation of an EIS, an agency must consider direct, indirect, and cumulative impacts (40 CFR §1508.25). EPA and its delegated state agencies (not to mention other federal agencies that also are subject to NEPA) must pay closer attention to the explicit inclusion of these environmental justice issues. In 1997, the Council on Environmental Quality directed federal agencies to consider environmental justice issues in the EIS process. Agencies must consider relevant public health data and industry data concerning the potential for multiple exposures or cumulative exposure to human health.

Methods for analyzing cumulative effects include: (1) carrying capacity analysis, (2) ecosystem analysis, and (3) social impact analysis. The carrying capacity analysis method identifies thresholds (as constraints on development) and provides mechanisms to monitor the incremental use of unused capacity. Carrying capacity in the ecological context is defined as the threshold of stress below which populations and ecosystem functions can be sustained. In the social context, the carrying capacity of a region is measured by the level of services (including ecological services) required by the community. The strengths of this method are that it is a true measure of cumulative effects against a threshold, it addresses the effects in a system context, and it addresses time factors. Its weaknesses are that it is currently difficult to measure this kind of capacity directly, there may be multiple thresholds, and this type of regional information in the United States often is not developed.

Ecosystem analysis explicitly addresses biodiversity and sustainability issues. It uses natural boundaries (*e.g.*, watersheds) and applies ecological indicators.[3] Ecosystem analysis entails a broad regional perspective. Its strengths are that it uses regional scale and addresses a large range of ecological interactions (including synergy, antagonism, and catalysis), addresses time, and seeks sustainability. Its current weaknesses are that it is limited to natural systems, requires more data than currently available, and some of the landscape indicators are still under development.

Social impact analysis addresses cumulative effects related to sustainability of human communities by focusing on variables such as demographics, community and institutional structures, political, social, and economic resources. It projects future effects using social analysis techniques such as linear trend projections. Its strengths are that it addresses social issues, and that the models provide definitive, qualified results. Its weaknesses are that utility and accuracy of results are dependent on data quality and model assumptions, and that social values are highly variable over time.

An engaged community with capacity could select a combination of the above factors that would tailor a community assessment to their place and their people. These methods can capture unintended consequences and impacts of urban environmental policy interventions, such as population displacement. Local populations, public health practitioners, and government officials should be well informed about 'the whole picture,' not just the one redevelopment site under consideration.

---

[3] See *Environmental Indicators: A Systematic Approach to Measuring and Reporting on Environmental Policy Performance in the Context of Sustainable Development*, World Resources Institute 1995

FINDING #5: Redevelopment projects lacked neighborhood demographic assessment to provide a more comprehensive understanding of adverse environmental and social impacts.

A neighborhood demographic assessment is important to EPA's fulfillment of its responsibilities under several executive orders that relate to environmental justice, including Executive Orders 12898 (Federal Actions to Address Environmental Justice in Minority Populations and Low-Income Populations) and 13116 (Limited English Proficiency), and related legal responsibilities under Title VI of the Civil Rights Act of 1964. Place study analyses can alert EPA to the possibility of disproportionate burdens and/or potentially adverse effects. A neighborhood demographic assessment also is important to EPA because it can assist in tracking cumulative impacts, protecting the environment, and reducing public health risk to vulnerable populations. A neighborhood demographic assessment can lay the foundation for new environmental policies like sustainability and inform environmental decisions in revitalization areas. A neighborhood demographic assessment recognizes the importance of community and culture in a particular place.

RECOMMENDATION #5: When appropriate, EPA should encourage an initial neighborhood demographic assessment and a projected impact assessment regarding displacement at the earliest possible time in a redevelopment or revitalization project. A similar assessment at the project's end should be carried out to measure changes and assess impacts. Such assessments may be facilitated as a requirement for EPA grant applications.

The goal of this assessment is to better understand early on who may be at risk of displacement and where the potential for gentrification could be expected as a result of demolition and/or rebuilding. The process also should examine which local businesses may be displaced through the redevelopment effort.

The assessment should be done by the developers and reviewed by local residents and stakeholders. EPA could help by providing assistance and U.S. Census data expertise. The process should be fully open to the community/neighborhoods. This could include a series of public meetings to ensure ample opportunities to learn about, observe, and participate in such a process. This process would build trust and assist all parties with understanding the Census data. Such an assessment also should track data not available from the Census, such as the homeless, new residents, seasonal migrant residents, and other undercounted subpopulations. The under- or non-counted residents may be those most likely to be displaced.

Likewise, smaller local businesses are more likely to be undercounted and thus under represented in assessing and protecting their displacement. These business owners are more likely to be unable to attend planning meetings, grant assistance workshops, proposal hearings, etc. These workers and business owners include restaurants, home daycare providers, repair shops, and convenience stores. These businesses are least likely to afford newer, more expensive commercial redevelopment properties. These businesses should be identified and counted early on in the process by the local residents and clients who are familiar with them. This kind of assessment can help prevent, and at least better record, gentrification on the commercial side.

EPA should develop a process and/or guidelines to support these demographic assessments for all of its redevelopment efforts. The process should start with the review of the most recent Census data. The assessment should enhance, with the help of stakeholders, the Census data regarding the undercounted. Stakeholders will know which 'businesses' will be mostly impacted. The assessment may require door-to-door surveys, which could be carried out by the stakeholders and residents. Developers should pay the cost of these assessments.

Specific measures for a potentially impacted pre-defined area include:
- Number of residential renters and owners;
- Number of rental units and owner occupied homes;
- Mean and median incomes;
- Mean and median housing/rent costs;
- Number of unofficial businesses (daycare, repair, cleaning, etc.) and who they serve;
- Estimates for homeless in area of attention;
- Business located in residential neighborhoods,
- Number of locally employed workers - those living and working within a given distance of redevelopment area; and
- Any other measures that are of concern regarding undercounting via the more traditional methods of counting.

County tax assessors have some of this data. Local school districts, health clinics, public service entities and churches may be helpful in providing more accurate demographic information as well. After the demographic assessment, EPA should support and facilitate a comprehensive review and adverse impact assessment. As a result, the community would have a better understanding of who is most likely to be adversely, and perhaps unintentionally, impacted via the redevelopment project. This knowledge would provide more lead-time to prevent, minimize or mitigate 'unintentional' adverse impacts.

FINDING #6: **The lack of state, tribal, and federal environmental agencies participation in local land use planning process has created an environment that fosters adverse unintended impacts such as displacement and gentrification.**

As resources decrease, it is important that local, tribal, state and federal agencies work effectively together in areas such as brownfields redevelopment and revitalization and other land use processes. For example, it is noted in the Cherokee Nation place study that the Oklahoma Department of Environmental Quality performed a Targeted Brownfields Assessment at the Chilocco Indian School Lands for the tribes who jointly own the land. Collaborating on such efforts allow for more effective use of resources. Similarly, as tribes develop response programs, lessons learned from other entities could allow tribes to avoid similar difficulties and assist with the development of tribal response programs.

Past efforts show when tribal, local and state interests work together, positive results can occur. For example, Cherokee Nation cross-deputization agreements with local law enforcement provide more resources and manpower for overall law enforcement. Likewise, the Cherokee Nation brings millions of dollars into Northeastern Oklahoma every month through tourism, business development, and job creation. The Cherokee Nation then reinvests the money in the area, creating new businesses and employing more than 4,000 people.

RECOMMENDATION #6: **State, tribal, and federal environmental agencies should be encouraged to find creative ways to participate in local land use planning, process, and government. For example, where state and/or federal permits apply, conditional permit issuance may be encouraged.**

It was observed that engagement in local land use planning and decision-making to better mitigate negative consequences of local zoning decisions and achieve environmental success falls outside of EPA's authority. Fully respecting that zoning decisions are made at the local level, EPA and state environmental agencies would do well to more actively track resource zoning considerations. For example, EPA and state environmental agencies can provide relevant environmental information about locations of contaminated sites and sources of pollution. This would provide a better understanding of those cumulative environmental impacts that may trigger zoning law provisions. An example of this is the establishment or enhancement of buffer zones between industrial and residential properties.[4] Lack of this type of intergovernmental support to urban redevelopment and revitalization projects may otherwise minimize community goals of such projects and possibly exacerbate other gentrifying forces present.

Ideally, as soon as a local planning commission in a redevelopment area receives any application for a land use change, notice of that change should go to the state environmental agency, and, perhaps, the EPA regional office. EPA should encourage local, tribal and state interests to work together, whenever possible, to make the best use of available resources to better understand and apply environmentally-sound land use decisions. The NEJAC previously has made a recommendation on the issue of intergovernmental cooperation in the report *Ensuring Risk Reduction in Communities with Multiple Stressors: Environmental Justice and Cumulative Risks/Impacts* (2004) which calls on government agencies at every level "[t]o address and overcome programmatic and regulatory fragmentation within the Nation's environmental protection regime."

CONCLUSION

This report represents a serious effort to highlight the challenging dynamics surrounding community revitalization efforts associated with brownfields redevelopment. The report cites efforts, paid for and led by EPA OSWER, that have contributed to both positive and negative outcomes. As would be expected, the adverse impacts associated with EPA's work have been unintentional. In many respects, these adverse impacts are due to factors far beyond EPA's control. However, they are not necessarily beyond EPA's ability, through funding decisions, oversight, coordination, effective listening and communication, and other means, to constructively influence or mitigate. While EPA may not have an official role or jurisdiction in issues of local zoning, it can still engage by sharing information, actively identifying relevant environmental considerations, and commenting to the local forums involved.

---

[4] See National Academy of Public Administration, *Addressing Community Concerns: How Environmental Justice Relates to Land Use Planning and Zoning* (July 2003).

This report seeks to provoke thinking about how to avoid or minimize unintended adverse impacts at redevelopment and revitalization sites. For example, EPA OSWER may find additional opportunities for avoiding unintended impacts by putting additional time and resources into tracking and understanding demographic dynamics in redevelopment and revitalization projects. Additionally, the NEJAC feels that it is important to empower community groups to take a greater role in the redevelopment and revitalization process. Such efforts may include assuming the role of developer. Such efforts can be very effective in bringing the additional skills and information needed for meaningful participation in brownfields decisions to impacted neighborhoods. The NEJAC urges that EPA view them as opportunities to listen, learn, and build on its many successes to make community redevelopment and revitalization in environmental justice communities even better.

Of equal importance, the NEJAC challenges EPA to avoid the collective urge to marginalize the report because of specific points that may seem unreasonably critical, overly complex, beyond current policies and procedures, or simply new. Rather, as much as possible, the report's findings and recommendations can be used in pursuit of furthering excellence. The NEJAC urges EPA to publish and circulate the report in the many communities and stakeholder groups where EPA is investing its time and money. EPA should use the report to help frame more questions and formulate responses. EPA should give these challenges the time and effort they deserve and demand. Finally, EPA should continue to solicit constructive counsel on these issues from the NEJAC and utilize the wealth of expertise within its members.

Unless we, as a Nation, accept the premise that an unavoidable cost for the revitalization of poor and decaying brownfields communities is the displacement of poor populations, we need to begin developing ways to integrate and reward sustained participation in such a process. While HAZMAT cleanup job training programs help provide employment for some residents during the cleanup and remediation phases of a revitalization project, more needs to be done to protect the equity stake that residents have in the community once the site is remediated and redeveloped. Our study findings indicate that this is a vitally important issue for homeowners, tenants and local small businesses.

There is no question that revitalized urban neighborhoods are good for the Nation's cities and that there will always be a cost for such revitalization. As these projects expand into more and more urban centers, EPA should maintain a close watch for patterns of disproportionate reward-sharing and cost-bearing in environmental justice communities. It is central to the notion of environmental justice that no population bears a disproportionate exposure to environmental hazards. In the same spirit, no population should consistently pay a disproportionate price for the cleanup and revitalization of the neighborhoods in which they live.

Community leaders and residents know that EPA cannot 'do it all,' easily change common practices from the past, or single-handedly make these problems go away. This is particularly true in cases where EPA has no authority. However, the many stakeholders who have shared their experiences on the unintended impacts of redevelopment and revitalization hope that their concerns will be heard, respected, and addressed. They do so for the sake of many others around the country in similar circumstances.

APPENDIX
PLACE STUDY SUMMARIES

The dynamics of actual and/or perceived impacts of redevelopment and revitalization projects on environmental justice communities make up the heart of this report. Each place study author examined available information, conducted interviews, and analyzed results consistent with the goals of the Work Group. Each of the place study summaries below briefly describes the background, situational dynamics, and analysis of unintended impacts for each location.

East Palo Alto, California

Incorporated in 1983, East Palo Alto, California has a population of nearly 30,000. Before incorporation, annexation of land around East Palo Alto left the city with few opportunities for industrial and commercial development. As a result, East Palo Alto is largely residential. Due to a severely inadequate tax base, the city struggled to provide essential city services, public facilities, and infrastructure for its largely poor, minority residents. According to the 2000 Census, non-whites make up at least 77.6% of East Palo Alto's population. From 1990 to 2000, the Latino population doubled in size. Meanwhile, the African-American population decreased by one-third.

A considerable portion of East Palo Alto's land can be considered brownfields, mostly because of soil contamination from old agricultural uses such as greenhouses, former and current chemical processing plants, auto wrecking and salvage yards, abandoned gas stations, machine shops, and other light industrial uses. Because of East Palo Alto's relatively small size (2.5 square miles), redevelopment and revitalization efforts generally have focused on the community at large. The city desperately needed affordable housing for existing local residence as well as cleanup programs to improve health and quality of life for these same residents.

From the latter half of the 1990s to the present, several federal agencies, with EPA in the lead, have invested funds, time and expert staff to East Palo Alto's revitalization work. This work is expected to continue in the future. By nearly all accounts, these resources have been very helpful to the community (city, residents, local businesses, and developers). Redevelopment efforts have built new housing for low-income and 'market-rate' residents on remediated sites. Redevelopment efforts also have resulted in the establishment of local businesses, a community park, and a public health clinic on brownfields properties. This support required comprehensive knowledge of key players, bureaucratic dynamics, and environmental justice concerns. None of those interviewed suggested these efforts have not had positive benefits for the city. For the most part, the invested work and time have been considered a success for both local stakeholders and for the many institutions that have contributed to this joint effort.

Specifically, for about the past four years, a full-time environmental/community involvement expert has been paid by EPA and 'loaned' to the City of East Palo Alto to help coordinate the City's needs related to its many clean-up and redevelopment activities. These activities have included applying for grants, conducting public outreach, and facilitating interagency coordination. The consistent finding from the East Palo Alto assessment was that EPA's contribution of a full-time, knowledgeable, and dedicated staff to the city government has made the complicated redevelopment processes work better and faster. Without this resource, the odds of the City's achieving its current successes would have been significantly diminished.

Albina Community, Portland, Oregon

The Albina Community consists of 15 neighborhoods in north and northeast sections of Portland, Oregon. The total population is more than 70,000. The Albina Community Plan, a long-term strategy, developed by citizens, business, and the city, defines Albina's neighborhood boundaries. The Albina community contains 17% of Portland's total population, and 39% of the total people of color in the city. Many people of color in Albina are African Americans, with growing populations of Latino, Native, and Asian Americans. The African American community is concentrated in Albina, where there has been brownfields redevelopment activity. This community is diverse and rich in history. It has a large number of community assets such as strong religious and civic organizations, support systems for children, and access to parks and recreational facilities.

The City of Portland has been awarded two brownfields grants, both premised on the cleanup of waste sites and community involvement. The latter brownfields grant was awarded to Portland as a Brownfields Showcase Community. Tri-Met, the regional transportation authority, also was involved in providing technical assistance. When Portland was awarded the Showcase award in 1998, city officials asked the north/northeast neighborhood to form a Community Action Council (CAC). The CAC held three community forums. After interested property owners delivered presentations on their site, the CAC voted on which sites to recommend for publicly funded assessments. These decisions resulted in a general shift of grant money away from southwest Portland to north/northeast Portland. Three applications were selected from the seven applications submitted by local property owners. Portland later determined that an extensive site assessment and selection process was not cost effective. Few proposals for assessment were submitted. Most of the property owners did not seek assessment because they perceived remediation as out of their reach due to limited access to capital, lack of development expertise, fear of liability, fear of reporting requirements, and distrust of local government.

Currently, the City of Portland is trying to communicate that many of the brownfields sites are not as contaminated as perceived, and that cleanup is possible. They no longer focus on north/northeast Portland, but have an open door policy for proposals from the entire city. Recent brownfields efforts are designed to stimulate an increase in mixed-use development in the city while preventing urban sprawl. Redevelopment efforts along the waterfront seek to improve water quality, preserve open spaces, and create new jobs and housing.

Recent revitalization efforts in the Albina community were based on the 1989 version of Portland's strategy to revitalize inner north/northeast Portland, formerly called "the Northeast District Plan" and renamed the Albina Community Plan. The area comprising the former city of Albina has been losing jobs, housing, population, and business since the 1950s. Public and private revitalization efforts were initiated. The North/Northeast Economic Development Task

Force, the Neighborhood Revitalization Program, and the shift to community policing all followed. The Task Force was to design an action plan to shape revitalization efforts.

The place study research and interviews indicate that it is too early to determine any trends. The community group felt that very few sites were actually redeveloped and that expectations were misrepresented. While most interviewees felt that Portland has serious gentrification problems, it was too early to say whether or not brownfields redevelopment was a factor. Sites have not been touched. As one community leader stated, "This was a promise, not a project." On the positive side, one community leader did feel that the project "…created a vehicle for community involvement committees in other processes. We learned how to do it from brownfields and have applied it to, for example, transportation." She further felt that there is a need to look at unintended consequences because community people went into this process with promises that could not be delivered. The Portland Bureau of Housing and Community Development used brownfields funds to build community groups and identify sites, but not to conduct remediation.

Washington Navy Yard, Washington, D.C.

Located within two miles of the White House, the Washington Navy Yard is the oldest operating naval facility in the United States. The facility is surrounded by substantially minority communities. The Anacostia River separates the communities of Southeast Washington, D.C. and Anacostia. Anacostia community residents believe that historically they have been neglected. The river separating the community from the rest of D.C. proper is both a symbolic and geographic dividing line. This situation was and is an important consideration for the Navy in establishing public outreach programs associated with the installation.

The Navy Yard is a gaining facility under the U.S Department of Defense (DoD) Base Realignment and Closure (BRAC) program. Specifically, this means that the Navy Yard received jobs and funding diverted from the closure and/or relocation of selected DoD facilities. In January 1997, the Navy completed a BRAC Construction Environmental Investigation that analyzed samples taken from soils, groundwater, and inside buildings. The view of the Navy is that there are no areas of concern located in the BRAC areas except for Site 6, the incinerator area, which was handled as a removal action during the summer of 1998. In addition to the BRAC-related cleanup action, the Navy Yard is in the target area for the Anacostia Waterfront Revitalization Project, and the city of Washington, D.C. also is involved in several HUD 6 revitalization projects in close proximity to the Navy Yard.

The Navy Yard project has generated some controversy. The Anacostia Watershed Society sought to have the Navy Yard conduct a cleanup along the Anacostia River, and, in conjunction with other partners, filed suit against the Navy Yard to conduct a cleanup. The surrounding community also has raised environmental justice concerns regarding the Navy Yard cleanup. In response, the Navy established a Restoration Advisory Board to facilitate community relations and to address environmental justice concerns. The board has met monthly and provided a forum for citizens to participate in the investigation and remediation processes.

The cleanup process included an assessment of the human health and ecological risks for the surrounding community and the environment. The Navy also established the "Bridges to

Friendship Program" to provide opportunities for the community to get involved in the process and leverage economic and quality of life opportunities presented by various funding programs. Bridges to Friendship is a highly regarded outreach program that received high praise from all parties involved including community members. The Navy also considered training and employing local residents for site-related cleanup activities. Environmental groups including the Sierra Club and the Anacostia Watershed Society have been working with the Chesapeake Bay Program Office, the Navy, and EPA to develop a supplemental environmental project that would benefit the community. All but one person interviewed for this place study answered "very beneficial" when asked how they assess the project's overall impact on the local community. Navy outreach programs benefited from the strong leadership exhibited by the Washington Navy Yard commander.

While outreach activities and Navy leadership were noteworthy, these programs achieved lower than expected success rates. This dynamic was mostly due to the community being unprepared to leverage opportunities and the government's inability to provide greater assistance due to bureaucratic atrophy and entrenchment among federal and local agencies, turf issues, and personalities. Additionally, local nonprofits lacked the necessary capacity to take advantage of the revitalization process.

While the environmental justice complaint was addressed, the perception of the outcome varied among different stakeholder groups. The Navy Yard cleanup project involved a considerable amount of public outreach, but these efforts met with limited success due to a number of factors. Most prominently, the multiple projects and grant programs undertaken in and around the Navy Yard involve many agencies, funding programs, and bureaucracies. From the community's perspective, the series of projects is one continuous set of activities with unclear lines of responsibility exacerbated by bureaucratic inertia, while the government agencies and developers involved in the effort tend to view the projects as separate and unrelated. These dynamics left unintended negative consequences. For example, the lack of synergy in government-sponsored public outreach often left communities unable to determine how to leverage available opportunities.

Cherokee Nation in Oklahoma

The Cherokee Nation Brownfields Assessment Pilot Project has focused on completing environmental site assessments (ESA) undertaken on four property areas by the Cherokee Nation Environmental Programs Group's Office of Environmental Services (OES). The project completion date was September 30, 2003. The Cherokee Nation also was selected to receive additional funding for the assessment of the Sequoyah High School landfill, an area adjacent to the Cherokee Nation's Pow-Wow grounds, to be used for green space purposes. The Pilot initially focused on the Cherokee Nation Hog Farm, the Cherokee Nation Landfill, and the Chilocco Indian School Lands. Chilocco Indian School Lands and the Cherokee Nation Landfill sites were deleted from the site list, and the Catoosa Truck Stop and the West Siloam Springs sites were later added to the list.

Activities and goals that were part of this Pilot included:

- Conducting Phase I and Phase II environmental assessments on targeted sites;
- Forming a Brownfields Advisory Committee, comprised of tribal and community leaders, state and federal officials, representatives of nonprofit organizations, developers, and other interested parties;
- Conducting economic redevelopment studies on a site-specific basis to evaluate possible site reuses; and
- Identifying additional federal, state, and private funding sources to redevelop brownfields sites.

EPA Region 6 has been involved in the pilot project in an oversight capacity pertaining to the operation of the grant.

Currently, the Cherokee Nation is a recipient of funding under Section 128(a) of the Comprehensive Environmental Response, Compensation and Liability Act (CERCLA). Section 128(a) seeks to enhance state and tribal response programs. The Cherokee Nation Brownfields Pilot established the framework for the response program.

Public involvement in the Cherokee Nation response program and other efforts is an integral part in ensuring successful environmental protection endeavors. Similar to other tribes throughout the country, the Cherokee Nation is a partner in communities throughout northeastern Oklahoma. A successful Cherokee Nation Brownfields Program is a win for the Cherokee Nation and its community partners.

Pensacola, Florida

The residential neighborhoods examined in this place study were condemned and EPA, as a part of the Escambia Wood Treating Company (ETC) Superfund Site Permanent Relocation Program, permanently relocated the families. Additionally, the program was designated a National Superfund Permanent Relocation Pilot. The purpose of this designation was to conduct the relocation. At the same time, EPA sought to draw lessons for the development of updated Regulation and Guidance for similar EPA projects in the future.

These subdivisions were built at a time when strict segregation laws were in force in the City of Pensacola, Florida. During this era, professional and blue collar African-American families who wanted to escape unfavorable conditions in the Pensacola's ghettos and build their own single-family homes had to buy land and build in unincorporated Escambia County. At the time, building your own subdivision was preferable to, and certainly safer than, trying to integrate into one of Pensacola's white neighborhoods. In terms of education, employment, and income, the families that built these subdivisions were considered the elites among Pensacola's African American population. The first of these enclaves sprang up in the 1930s in what is now called "Goulding/Herman's Plat." Most of the homes in the Oak Park and Rosewood subdivisions were constructed between 1956 and 1961. During this period, the privately owned Escambia Arms Apartments, a Section-8 Certified, 200-unit complex, also was built.

The land available for purchase was located adjacent to two existing industrial facilities. Until they ceased operations, the Escambia Treating Company (1942-1982) and the Agrico Chemical

Company (1889-1975) provided a significant level of employment for the wage earners in these African American settlements. Although the "founding" families attempted to buy land that was not next to an industrial facility, anecdotal evidence indicates that no such option was available at the time.

In consultation with the Florida Department of Environmental Protection (FDEP), EPA began a removal action of PCP/Dioxin-contaminated sludge and soils at the ETC site in 1991. The 225,000 cubic yards of contaminated excavated materials were subsequently (and are currently) stockpiled on site in a 60-foot tall "L"-shaped mound. Local and national environmental justice activists almost immediately dubbed this huge mound of contaminated material "Mount Dioxin." This site was listed on the national priorities list (NPL) in December 1994. After an extensive remedial site inspection, EPA issued a Record of Decision (ROD) titled *Interim Remedial Action and National Relocation Pilot Project Escambia Treating Company Site Pensacola, Escambia County, Florida* on February 12, 1997. After the Love Canal (Niagara Falls, New York) and Times Beach (Missouri) relocations, Pensacola represents the third largest relocation ever conducted by EPA.

In order to address their immediate issues and concerns, the residents formed a grass-roots organization called Citizens Against Contaminated Environments (CATE). Mrs. Margaret Williams, a resident of Goulding and a former schoolteacher, headed CATE. With assistance from the Southern Organizing Committee, Northwest Florida Legal Services, NEJAC, and TAG Grants from EPA, CATE and community residents, organized, educated themselves, and launched a highly visible and effective national campaign. This effort brought attention to their plight and ultimately secured needed remedies.

EPA contracted with the U.S. Army Corps of Engineers (USACE) to design and conduct the relocation program. Using the Uniform Relocation Assistance Act (URA) and the USACE's Guidance for Eminent Domain "takings" of condemned homes, the government appraised the homes, determined what they would offer for the purchase of the properties, disbursed sale proceeds and assisted in the relocation of the families. The very minimal relocation support services suggested by the URA were offered to relocating families. In addition, other payments defrayed relocation-related costs. The tenants of the Escambia Arms Apartment complex were given options for using their relocation benefits to become first-time homeowners.

The Pensacola place study highlights important unexpected impacts that reflect both positive and negative outcomes. It serves as a marvelous example of how an Agency can be open enough to listen carefully to citizens and flexible enough to incorporate significant changes into a program even while it is being implemented. The challenges that the Pensacola place study pose present EPA with an opportunity to find ways to work with the URA and develop policy and guidance documents that will better serve environmental justice communities in need of relocation. More detailed agreements and closer supervision of relocation vendors can ensure that EPA's vision for an effective and equitable relocation process will in fact materialize in the field.

www.ingramcontent.com/pod-product-compliance
Lightning Source LLC
Chambersburg PA
CBHW080930290526
45795CB00007BA/2697